DRAW PLUS MORE MATH

Enhance Math Learning Through Art Activities

by

Freddie Levin

Before you begin:

You will need:

a pencil

an eraser

paper (recycle and re-use!)

a folder to keep your work

a metric ruler

a compass for drawing circles or a circle template

a good light and a comfortable place to draw

Now let's begin!

Library of Congress CIP Data (original edition)

Levin, Freddie.
  Draw plus more math : enhance math learning
through art activities / by Freddie Levin.
     pages cm
  Includes index.
  Audience: Ages 9-13.
  Audience: Grades 4 to 6.
  ISBN: 9781725102385 (trade paper : alk. paper)
  1. Mathematics--Study and teaching (Elementary)
2. Early childhood education--Activity programs. 3.
Children's drawings. I. Title.
  QA135.6.L4785 2013
  372.3--dc23
                          2013000757

Contents

Drawing tips:

- Draw lightly at first. SKETCH, so you can easily erase extra lines later.

- Practice, practice, practice!

- Have fun with *Draw Plus More Math!*

To Teachers and Parents:

Welcome to Draw Plus More Math! This book is designed to help your child or student enhance math learning through art activities with exercises that supplement the study of math in a fun way. Recommended for Advance Elementary Math students, it is a continuation of Draw Plus Math at a more challenging level. Children learn through all of their senses. For visual and kinetic learners, concepts such as fractions and ratios are more accessible when presented as a drawing lesson. Learning to see patterns in art and nature is a mathematical skill. Symmetry reveals patterns that help organize the world.

The concepts presented include: radial and other symmetry, complex patterns, tangrams, tessellations, circles and triangles, geometric solids, simple fractals, ratio, scale and proportion, and the golden rectangle. The lessons are based on learning goals outlined by the Principles and Standards for School Mathematics, developed by the National council of Teachers of Mathematics (NCTM). For more information please access this website: http://standards.nctm.org.

Basic Shapes

These basic shapes will be used in drawings. Practice drawing these shapes. Use a straight edge or ruler, and a compass or circle template if you like. Metric measurements are used throughout this book. They can easily be converted to inches, if desired.

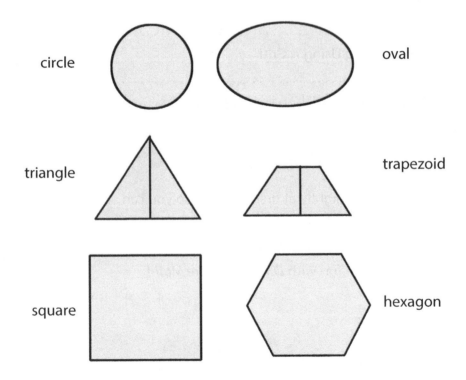

Symmetry
Bilateral Symmetry

When we think of SYMMETRY, we picture an object like a butterfly. A butterfly can be divided in half with a vertical line and each half will be a mirror image of the other. This is called BILATERAL (left-right) SYMMETRY.

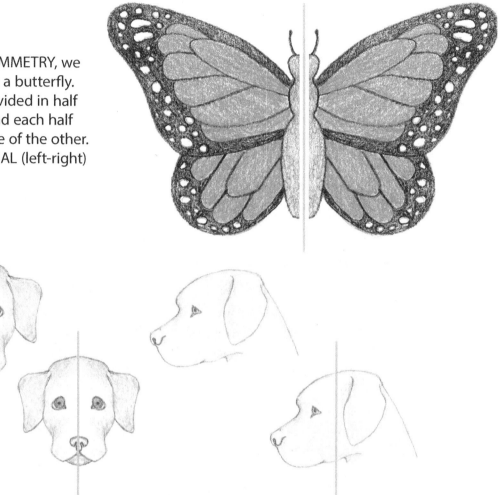

Some objects, like a dog's head, are symmetrical in one view and not the other. If you divide the object in half and the two halves aren't equal, the object isn't symmetrical. It is ASYMMETRICAL.

An object like a snowflake can be symmetrical in several ways. It can be divided in half vertically or horizontally. It can be divided along any AXIS. It has six lines of SYMMETRY.

Radial Symmetry

Mandala

Another kind of SYMMETRY is called RADIAL SYMMETRY. This is a design that radiates from a central point. Each section of the design, which is divided like an orange, is equal to its other sections. A design like this is sometimes called a MANDALA.

The word MANDALA is from the ancient language of Sanskrit. It means 'circle.'

Let's draw a MANDALA.

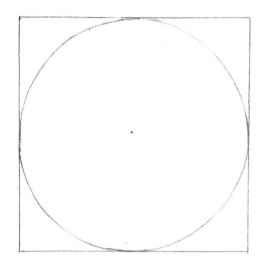

We'll start with a circle inside a square. Circles are difficult to draw so use a compass or trace the bottom of a round container. Use a ruler or straight edge for the straight lines.

Draw a VERTICAL and HORIZONTAL line to create the axis point.

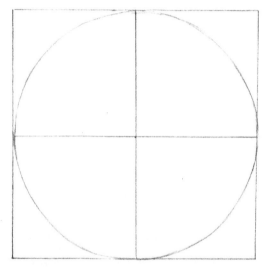

Draw two straight lines from corner to corner of the square. The circle is now divided into eight equal sections.

Whatever you draw in one section, you will repeat in all seven others.

Erase the lines of the square.

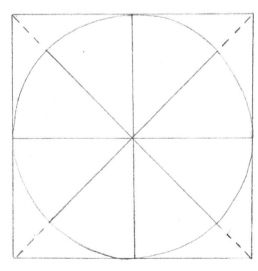

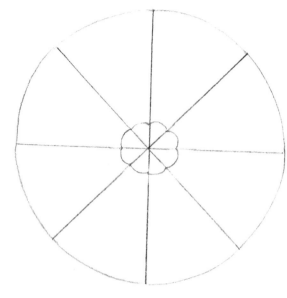

Draw a curved line near the center of each section of the MANDALA.

Draw a small circle in the very center of the design.

Using curved lines, add two leaf shapes and a circle in each section.

Continue to fill in one section of the circle with a design. You can follow this design, or you can make up a design of your own.

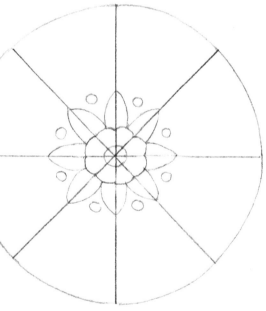

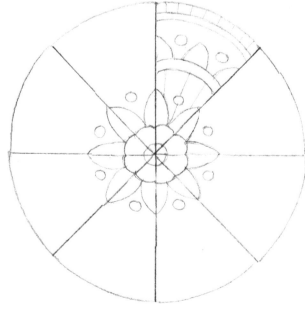

Just remember that what you draw in one section must repeat in all other sections as well.

Complete the pencil drawing.

Fill each section with color. You can alternate the colors for a more interesting pattern. Use whatever colors you like. The possibilities are endless.

Finish coloring your MANDALA.

Magnificent!

Flower

RADIAL SYMMETRY occurs frequently in nature. It is a common pattern for growth.

Let's draw two examples of RADIAL SYMMETRY: a flower and a sea star.

Start the flower with a bumpy circle.

Add a smaller bumpy circle inside the bigger circle.

Draw a dot in the middle.

Draw a petal on one side of the flower. Add another petal to the other side.

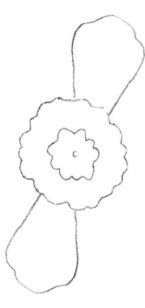

Add two more petals.

Draw four more petals.

Add short lines radiating out from the center.

Color your flower yellow.

Add shading.

Fine flower!

Sea Star

Draw a horizontal line. Add two more intersecting lines, crossing the first line at the center. Notice that the spaces between the lines are equal. Each section, just as is in the Mandala, is the same.

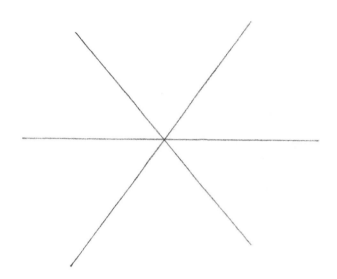

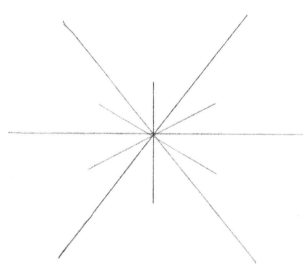

Add three more shorter lines that divide and cross the long lines. Notice that all the lines cross at the center. All sections of the design are equal in size.

Add two curving bumpy lines to form one leg of the sea star.

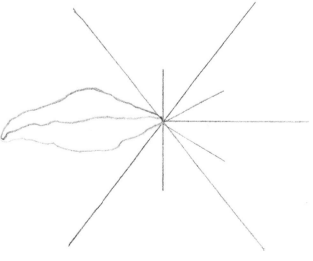

Add more curvy, bumpy lines to finish the eight legs.

Begin coloring your sea star

with a layer of orange.

Shade and color the sea star.

Do you see the RADIAL SYMMETRY?

Look around you. What can you find that has radial symmetry?

Make sketches of the objects.

Complex Symmetry

We organize what we see through symmetry and patterns. It's all around us in nature and design. There are four other important types of symmetry.

Let's explore them by starting with a simple design element, which we'll use in each of the patterns so that you can easily see the differences. If it seems a bit complicated at first, be patient because once you draw the patterns it will become clearer to you, and you will begin to see these types of patterns everywhere.

Draw a 2 cm long base line to start a triangle. Draw another 1 cm line for the height of the triangle. Add two more lines to complete the triangle.

Erase the vertical line in the center.

Draw a half circle.inside the triangle.

Color the design element using two contrasting colors.

Reflection

Reflection is a type of symmetry where one half is the reflection of the other half. Similar to BILATERAL SYMMETRY (see page 5), each unit of the pattern has a set direction and a set distance. We'll use a grid as a guide to help us keep the distance and position of each design element the same.

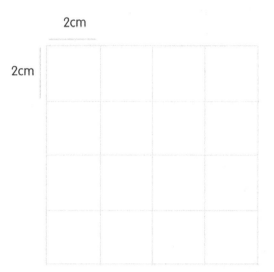

Step one: Draw a grid measuring 8 cm wide by 8 cm long. Draw lines across and down to make four 2 cm squares across and four 2 cm squares down on each grid. Sketch lightly so you can erase the lines later. It is only a guide for placing the design elements.

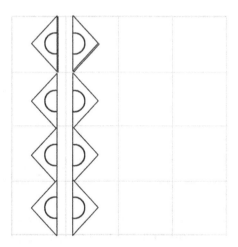

Step 2: Start with two vertical rows of triangles. Notice how they face each other as if they were reflected in a mirror. There are four triangles in each row and eight triangles all together.

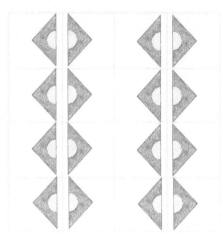

Step 3: Make one more pair of vertical reflecting rows. You have doubled the amount of triangles to sixteen.

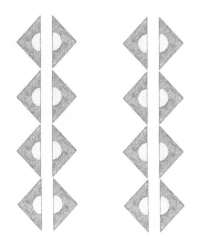

Step 4: Color the triangles and erase the guide lines of the grid.

Translation

TRANSLATION is a type of symmetry in which the position of an element can slide over and repeat without changing it in any other way. Each unit of the pattern has a set direction and a set distance. Let's make a pattern that shows TRANSLATION.

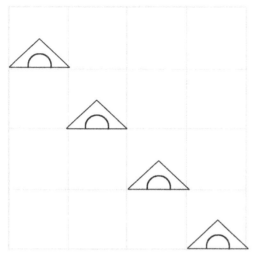

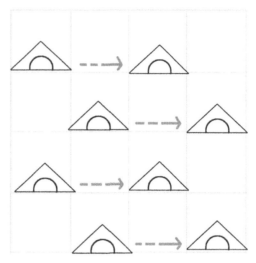

Step one: Draw a grid. Draw four triangles in the positions shown on the grid. The bottom line of the triangle rests on the bottom line of its individual square in the grid.

Step two: Add two more triangles to the grid as shown. Note that their position within their individual square has not changed but they have shifted one row over and one row down. The triangles still rest on the bottom line of their square.

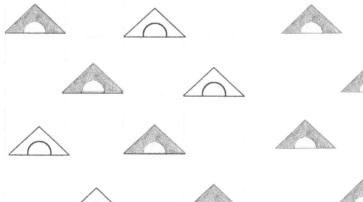

Step three: Repeat the pattern as shown, filling the rest of the grid. Every other square is blank.

Notice that in this symmetry pattern, nothing has changed but the position of the triangles. The

triangles have not rotated. Each triangle sits on the bottom line of its individual square but moves over and down within the grid.

Step four: Add color to the triangles. Erase the grid lines.

Glide Reflection Symmetry

A GLIDE symmetry is a pattern that combines REFLECTION and TRANSLATION. Each element moves in a line parallel to the translation (glide) and reflects the element. Let's create a pattern with this symmetry.

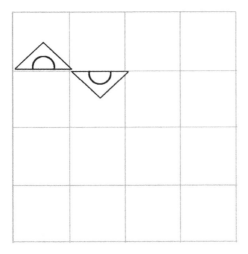

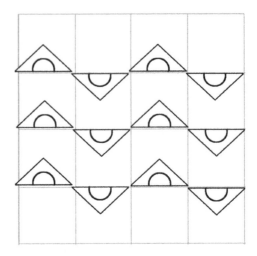

Sketch a grid with four squares across and four down. The first triangle design element sits on the bottom of the first top square. Draw it.

The next design element is upside down and sits on the top edge of its square. Draw it. Continue this pattern for three rows.

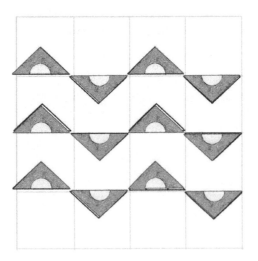

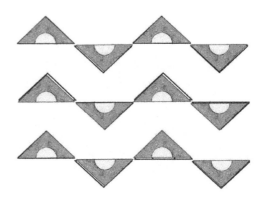

Color the triangles.

Erase extra grid guidelines.

Great glide!

16

Rotational Symmetry

In ROTATIONAL symmetry, each design element is the same, but it turns in equal amounts around a central axis. The distance between each element is the same. A familiar example of ROTATIONAL symmetry is the Recycling sign. Let's draw a design with ROTATIONAL symmetry.

Draw a grid. Place a dot in the center. Each triangle element will rotate around the red dot. The grid will help you place the elements at equal intervals.

Draw the first triangle design element as shown in the center of the grid. Add three more design elements. The pattern looks like a pinwheel.

Color your design.

Repeat the group of rotating elements to create a more complex pattern. These types of symmetry and patterns have endless variations.

Can you find examples of ROTATIONAL symmetry around you? Symbols on wrapping paper? Logos on products? They're everywhere.

Complex Patterns

To create more complex patterns, let's start with a bigger grid. This grid will still be divided into 2 cm by 2 cm squares, with eight squares across and eight squares down.

To create a repeating design element, let's focus on one piece of the grid – a square section of 2 cm by 2 cm.

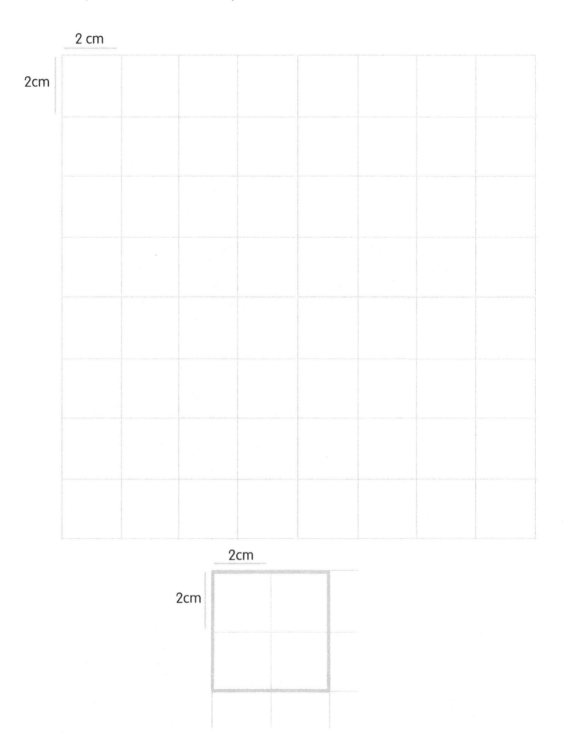

Let's use our original design element from page 13.

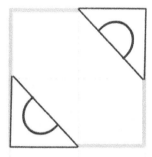

Draw two elements in two corners of the small grid section, facing each other.

Add two more elements in the other two corners. See how different our design looks when it is arranged this way.

Draw a circle in the center.

Color the outer design elements with two contrasting colors. Color the center.

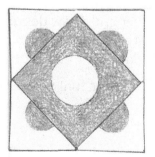

Draw another square and reverse the colors.

You now have two new design elements to place in the larger grid.

Look carefully at the alternating color designs in the grid. It looks like a checkerboard. Add these design elements to your grid.

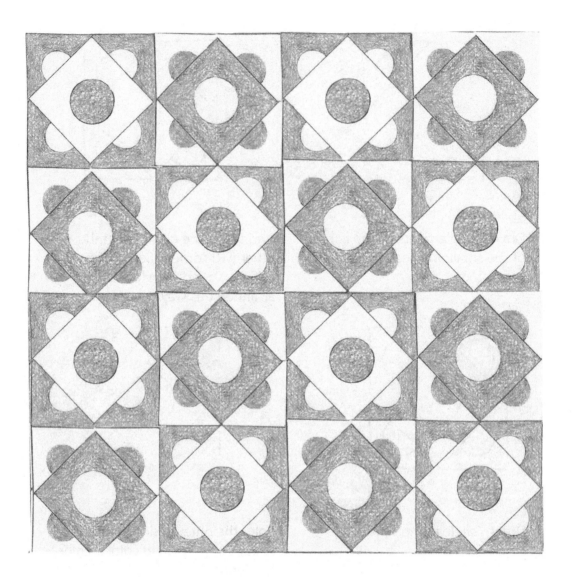

Draw another grid. Draw design elements at an angle to create a different edge.

EXPERIMENT! Have fun!

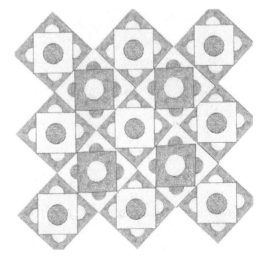

Patterns can also be made with pictures of objects. Let's make a pattern of fish and sea shells. First draw the fish.

Start with an oval. Add an eye.

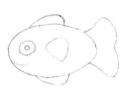

Add fins and a tail. Draw a mouth.

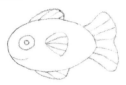

Draw fin rays on all the fins.

Color your fish.

For the sea shell, start with a rounded triangle.

Add two small triangles at the bottom.

Draw lines on the sea shell.

Color your sea shell.

Make a grid. Look at the design below. Draw the fish you see going different directions on the grid. Make one row going left and one row going right. Notice how the fish are positioned on the lines of the grid.

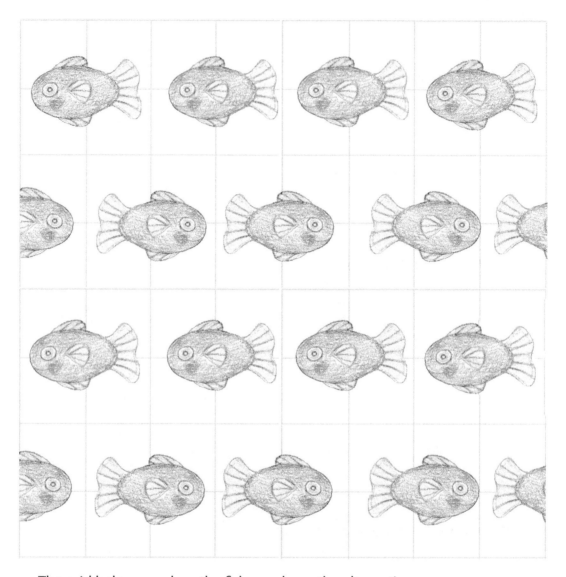

The grid helps you place the fish evenly on the alternating rows.

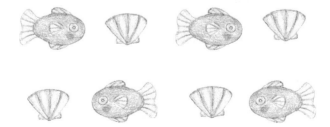

Draw another grid. Now try a pattern alternating fish and sea shells.

Introduce a third design element. Alternate fish and sea shells, and add circles to the pattern. One row of fish goes left and the next row of fish goes right.

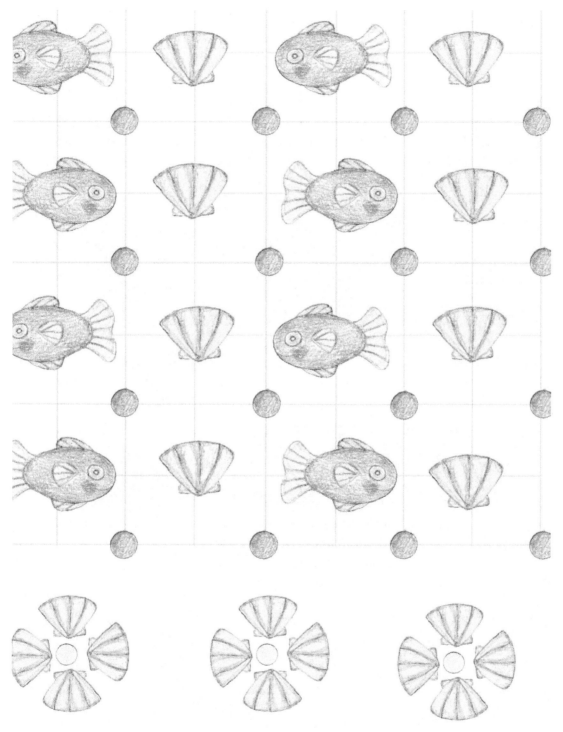

Draw more grids. Try a rotational pattern with sea shells. Repeat the design element.

Try some patterns and combinations of your own. Pattern possibilities are endless!

Geometric Shapes

Triangles

Geometric shapes follow exact mathematical rules. They are structured and precise. Let's start with a triangle and make new shapes out of it by repeating it in a pattern.

Start with a 2 cm horizontal line and a 3 cm vertical line.

Draw the sides of the triangle. It's important that the sides of the triangle measure the same length.

This is called an ISOSCELES (eye SOSS uh lees) triangle. Erase the vertical line and color the triangle.

Draw a triangle right side up and draw another triangle upside down.

Erase the inner line.

Your two triangle shapes have become a diamond shape. Color it.

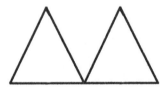

Draw two triangles next to each other.

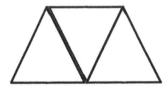

Add an upside down triangle in between. These combined shapes make a TRAPEZOID.

Color your TRAPEZOID.

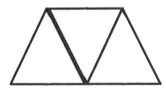

Draw the TRAPEZOID shape again.

Draw another one upside down. Erase the extra lines.

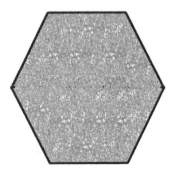

This shape, with six sides, is called a HEXAGON.

Play and experiment with triangles. What other shapes can be created?

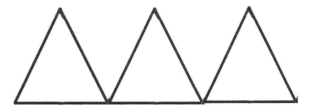

Let's make a more complicated shape out of triangles.

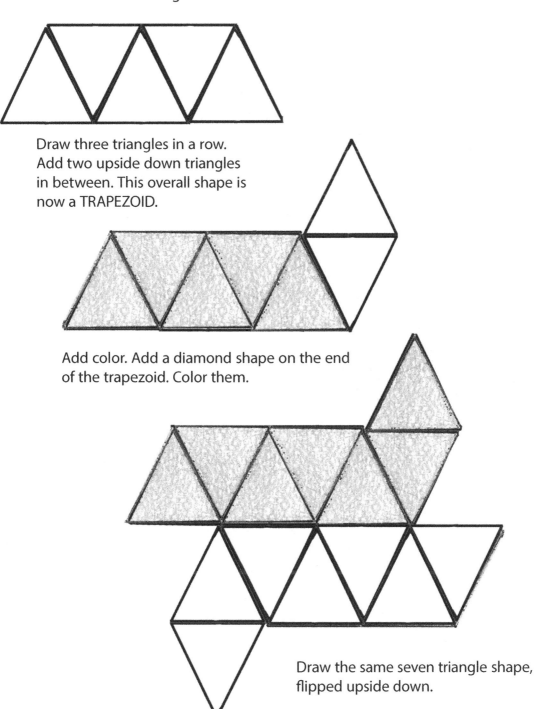

Draw three triangles in a row. Add two upside down triangles in between. This overall shape is now a TRAPEZOID.

Add color. Add a diamond shape on the end of the trapezoid. Color them.

Draw the same seven triangle shape, flipped upside down.

Add two more triangles.

Color them.

Again, add two more triangles,

then color them.

Erase extra lines and color the shape. This shape has ROTATIONAL SYMMETRY.

What other shapes can you make out of triangles? EXPERIMENT!

Circles

Patterns with circles have been used for centuries. Early examples of circle patterns have been found in ancient Egyptian temples and tombs.

Let's make some interesting patterns with OVERLAPPING circles. To draw circles, it is helpful to have a drawing compass and a circle template for tracing circles, or the bottom of a round container. The compass is best for this design because it's always clear where the center of the circle is located.

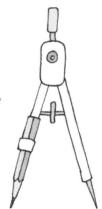

Start with a blue dot. This will be the center of your first circle. Draw a circle. Make all circles the same size.

Draw an overlapping circle. The edge of one touches the center of the other.

Repeat until you have four circles in a row.

Start another row of circles. The center of this next circle is where the first two circles intersect.

Add two more circles in this row. Notice where the center of the circles are in each.

28

Keep adding circles. The blue dots show where the point of the compass is placed.

Color your OVERLAPPING circle design with contrasting colors.

Awesome!

Tangrams

A TANGRAM is a very old Chinese math puzzle consisting of seven flat shapes, called tans. The objective is to fill an outline form using all seven shapes. The shapes must lay flat, and none may overlap.

Creating a TANGRAM is a great way to see the parts of a whole and to recognize the whole from its scattered parts.

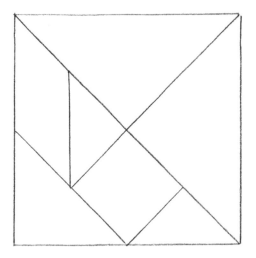

To make a tangram, start with a square. Draw lines to divide it into seven pieces.

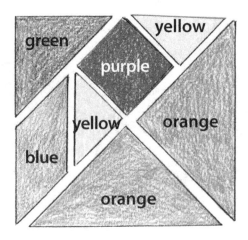

Look at the square and look at the shapes that are created when the square is divided.

Color code the pieces and name the shapes.

Orange: two large triangles

Green: one medium triangle

Yellow: two small triangles

Purple: one square

Blue: one parallelogram

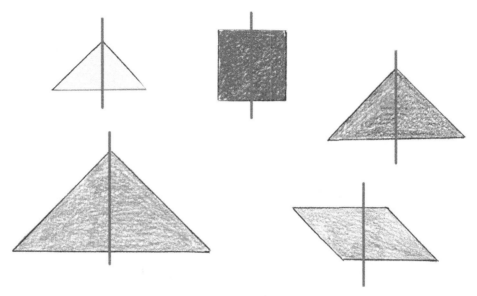

All the shapes are symmetrical except for the PARALLELOGRAM. A symmetrical triangle is called an ISOSCELES triangle. If all three sides are equal, it is called an EQUILATERAL triangle. Combining different pieces can create a new shape. For example, the two large orange triangles can be made into a square. The two yellow triangles can be combined to create a PARALLELOGRAM, a 4-sided flat shape with straight sides where opposite sides are parallel.

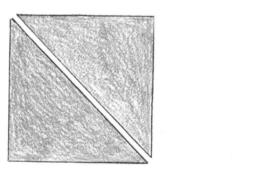

Let's make a tangram together. Draw a square on a separate piece of paper.

Divide it into the shapes you see pictured on page 30.

Color the shapes and cut them out.

Arrange and place the cut shapes back into the square.

Remember: they must lay flat, and not overlap other pieces.

Good job!

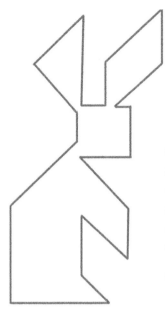

Let's make another TANGRAM shaped like a rabbit. Look at the outline. Draw it.

What shapes do you see? Color the square purple. Color the large triangle orange. Color the medium triangle green. Color the other big triangle orange.

Count the shapes.

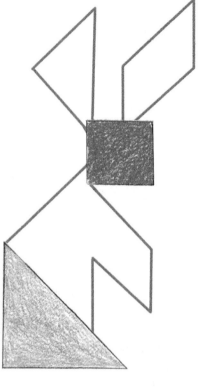

Only six? No problem, divide the top PARALLELOGRAM into two small triangles and color them yellow.

Now we have seven shapes.

Color the other PARALLELOGRAM blue.

Really nice rabbit!

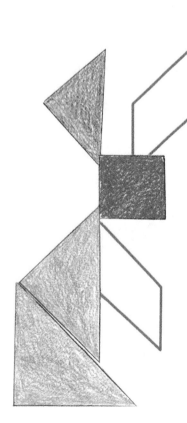

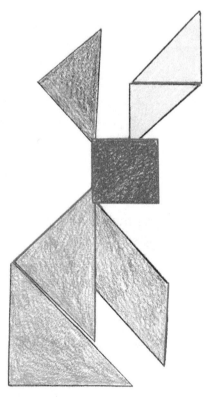

Let's make a TANGRAM in the shape of a SWAN.

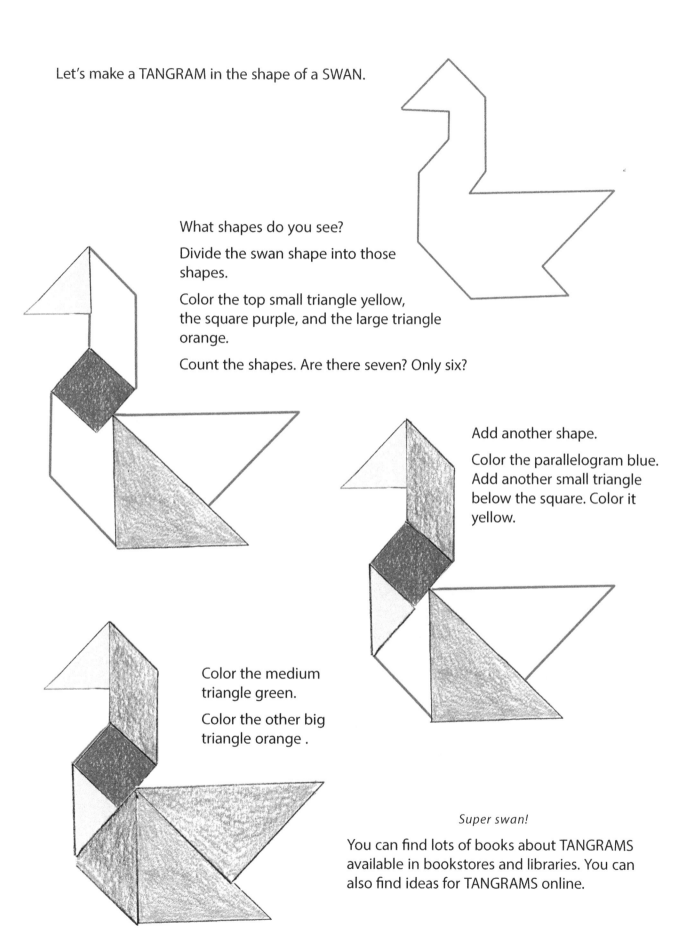

What shapes do you see?

Divide the swan shape into those shapes.

Color the top small triangle yellow, the square purple, and the large triangle orange.

Count the shapes. Are there seven? Only six?

Add another shape.

Color the parallelogram blue. Add another small triangle below the square. Color it yellow.

Color the medium triangle green.

Color the other big triangle orange .

Super swan!

You can find lots of books about TANGRAMS available in bookstores and libraries. You can also find ideas for TANGRAMS online.

Tessellations

A TESSELLATION is a pattern that is created when a shape is repeated over and over without overlapping or gaps.

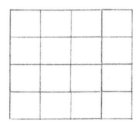 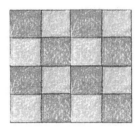

The simplest example of a TESSELLATION is a checkerboard. Regular TESSELLATIONS like these are also called TILING.

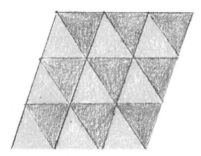

A variety of shapes can work as TESSELLATIONS. Here is an example using triangles. Notice, there's no overlapping or gaps between the triangles.

A VERTEX is the point where all the corners of a shape meet. Look at the diagrams. Each VERTEX must be the same.

The circle in the drawings below shows where the corners of the shapes meet.

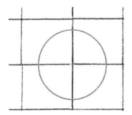 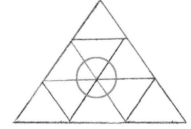

The shapes used in TESSELLATIONS must be regular geometric shapes or REGULAR POLYGONS. That means they can have three, four, five, or more sides, and all the angles are equal. They must also be SYMMETRICAL.

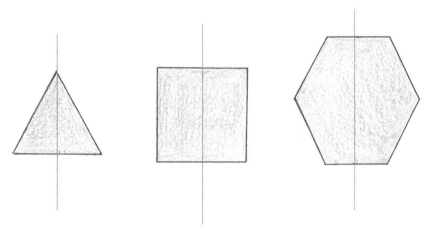

Three POLYGONS that work in REGULAR TESSELLATIONS are TRIANGLES (three sides), SQUARES (four sides), and HEXAGONS (six sides).

SEMI-REGULAR TESSELLATIONS combine more than one type of POLYGON. This is an example using triangles and hexagons.

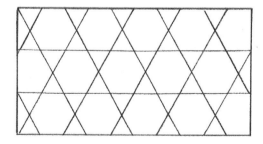 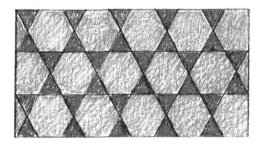

Let's make some TESSELLATIONS. We'll make one REGULAR and one SEMI-REGULAR. We'll see how color can make a difference as well.

You will need a ruler for measuring and for making straight lines.

35

Regular Tessellation

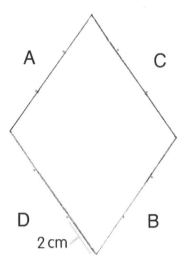
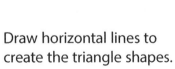

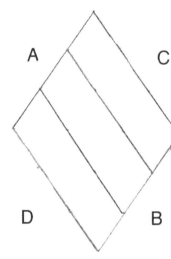

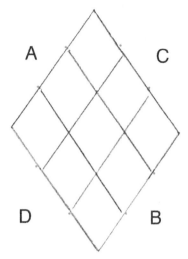

Start with a diamond shape. Make each side 6 cm long. With dots, mark off each 2 cm on all four sides.

Draw lines from side A to side B as shown.

Draw lines from side C to side D.

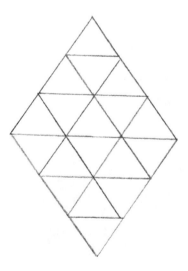

Draw horizontal lines to create the triangle shapes.

Color your REGULAR TESSELLATION.

Notice that shading can give it a different look.

Semi-Regular Tessellation

For this TESSELLATION, draw a rectangle. The width is 7 cm and the height is 8 cm. Look carefully at the measurements. Sides A and B are different from sides C and D. Measuring from the bottom up, mark off each side with dots as shown.

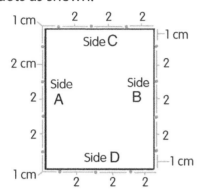 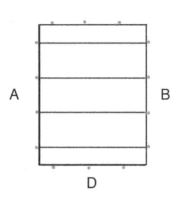

Side A and B: 1 cm, 2 cm, 2cm, 2 cm. Side C and D: 1 cm, 2 cm, 2cm

Draw horizontal lines from the dots on Side A to Side B.

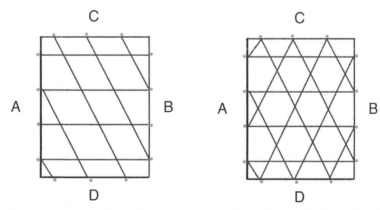

Draw the diagonal lines that slant from right to left, and left to right.

Contrasting colors in the triangle TESSELLATION makes a big difference in the appearance of the pattern. Try using different colors to change the look of the pattern.

TERRIFIC TESSELLATIONS!

Fractals

FRACTALS are very special geometric shapes that behave in interesting ways. Each small part of a FRACTAL is a little copy of the whole shape. FRACTALS start out with a simple shape that gets repeated and repeated, and every time it repeats, it gets a little smaller and a little more complicated. FRACTALS can be extremely complicated but we will draw a simple one made of triangles. It starts with one triangle.

Draw an 8 cm horizontal line.

Add a 7 cm vertical line.

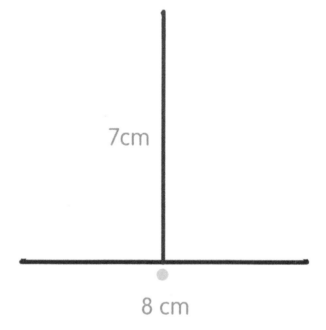

Draw straight lines to form the sides of the triangle.

Erase the vertical line. This is an 8 cm EQUILATERAL TRIANGLE. All three sides are the same, or EQUAL.

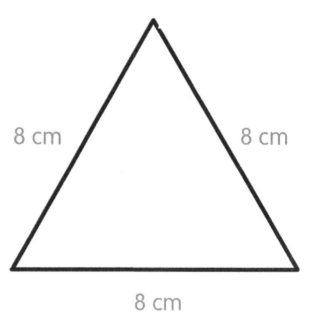

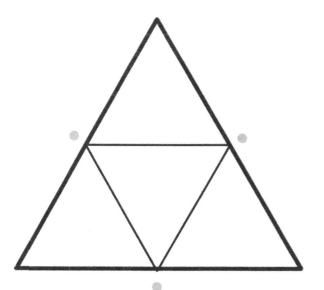

Place a dot at the middle of each side of the triangle. Draw lines to connect the three dots. We now have four smaller triangles inside the large one.

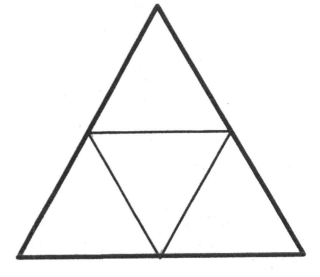

Color the three outside triangles with a light color.

The FRACTAL will become more complicated as added triangles become smaller and smaller. They are all still EQUILATERAL TRIANGLES.

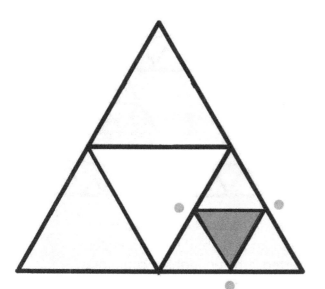

Measure the light-colored triangles. Place a dot at the middle of each side. Connect the dots with lines, creating three new smaller triangles.

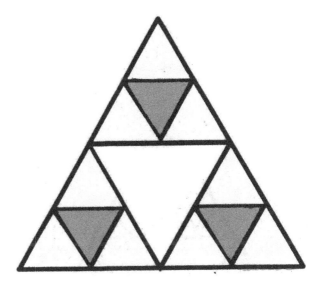

Make the new triangles a darker color. I used red, so I will call them red.

Measure again, halfway along the sides of the new darker (red) triangles.

Connect the dots with lines to create nine new and smaller triangles.

Color them a third color (I used blue). The new triangles have created 27 small triangles.

Divide the smaller (blue) triangles again, always starting in the middle of the line. Draw twenty-seven new triangles and color them another, darker color.

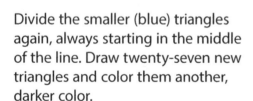

You could go on and on dividing the triangles into more and more triangles, if you started large enough, or could draw small enough. Each set would be tinier and more numerous but they would never change their basic shape. This trait is called SELF SIMILARITY.

Did you count the smallest triangles?

Fabulous FRACTA/LS!

Geometric Solids

Sphere

All the exercises so far have dealt with flat, two dimensional geometric shapes like triangles, circles, and hexagons. In this section, we will explore geometric shapes which have three dimensions: height, width, and depth. We call these GEOMETRIC SOLIDS.

Let's draw a circle and turn it into a SPHERE. A SPHERE is the shape of a ball or a globe.

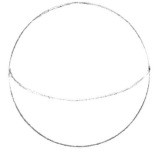

Draw a curved line in the middle of the circle. This shows that it's round.

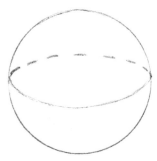

Draw a dashed curved line above the first curved line. This shows the inside curve of the SPHERE.

Practice shading half of a SPHERE. This is a bowl shape.

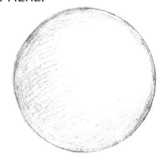

Finish shading the SPHERE to make it look round. Leave a white highlight on one side.

Shade your SPHERE with color. I used blue with a bit of purple for shadows.

Cylinder

A CYLINDER is the shape of a can or a tube.

To draw a CYLINDER start with an OVAL.

Draw two vertical lines from each end of the oval to form the sides.

Draw a curved line on the bottom of the CYLINDER.

Show the inside curve of the CYLINDER with a dashed line.

Shade your CYLINDER.

Cube

A CUBE is the shape of a box or block.

Draw a square to start.

3.5 cm

3.5 cm

3.5 cm

3.5 cm

A

To draw the CUBE in perspective, draw a HORIZON line with a blue dot on it. Label it "A".

Draw straight lines from A to connect with the outside points of B, D, and E.

B   D

C   E

A

Look carefully at the box shape emerging.

Measure 2 cm from F to G. Draw one vertical line from G to H. Draw one horizontal line from H to J to finish the back sides of the cube.

J   H

B   D

G

2 cm

E   F

Erase extra lines.

Shade and color your cube.

Pyramid

A PYRAMID is a three dimensional triangle. Some PYRAMIDS are three sided but we will draw a four sided PYRAMID.

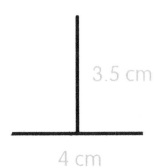

Start with a 4 cm horizontal line. Draw a 3.5 cm vertical line.

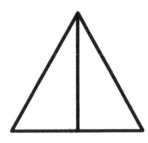

Draw two straight lines to shape the sides of the triangle.

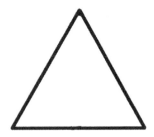

Erase the extra middle line.

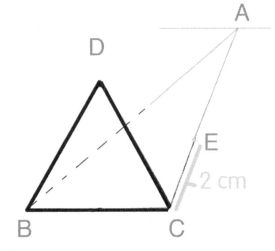

Just as in the CUBE on page 43, draw a horizon line and make a dot on it. Call it point A. Draw a line to connect C to A. Draw a line to connect B back to A. Measure 2 cm back from point C to mark point E.

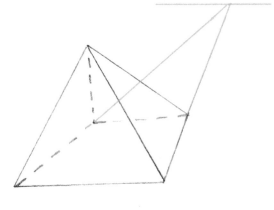

Draw a line to connect D to E. Show the inside of the PYRAMID with dashed lines.

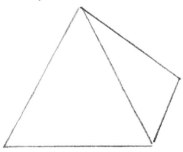

Erase extra lines.

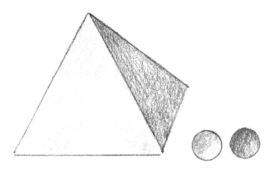

Shade and color your PYRAMID.

44

Scale

To make an accurate drawing of an object (large or small - like a building or a bug), artists make a SCALE DRAWING using actual measurements of the object 'SCALED' up or down, so that the drawing can fit on a piece of paper called a blueprint. The drawing is THE SAME in proportion to the actual object.

Lets's make a SCALE DRAWING of a 22 meter high robot. First we must decide on a RATIO in the drawing to compare it to the size of the real thing. For every meter of the robot's actual measurement, we use 1 cm in the drawing.

1 2 3 4 5

5 cm

5 centimeters equal
5 meters

5 cm = 5 meters

8 cm

Let's begin with the head.

The robot head is 5 meters by 5 meters. We will draw it in proportion.

In our drawing, the head is 5cm by 5cm.

The robot's eyes measure 1 meter by 1 meter. Make the eyes to scale on your drawing: 1 cm by 1 cm.

Make the mouth of your robot 3 cm by 5 cm. How big is the robot's actual mouth?

The body of the robot is 8 meters by 8 meters. The body in your small drawing is 8 cm by 8 cm.

Robot upper arms: 2 meters by 4 meters.

Drawing of upper arms: 2 cm by 4 cm.

Robot legs: 2 meters by 6 meters

Drawing of legs: 2 cm by 6 cm.

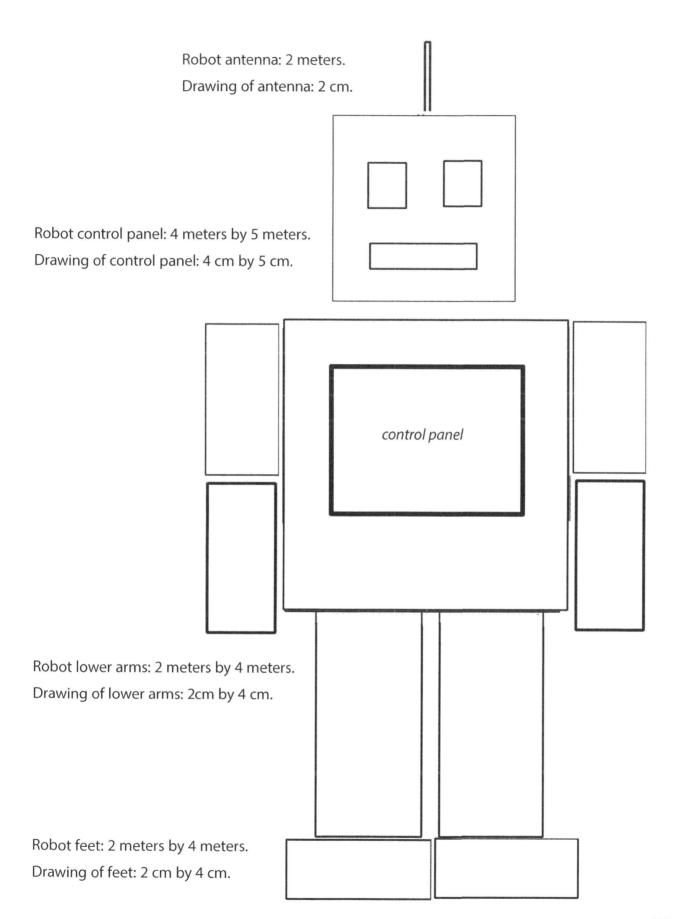

Robot antenna: 2 meters.
Drawing of antenna: 2 cm.

Robot control panel: 4 meters by 5 meters.
Drawing of control panel: 4 cm by 5 cm.

control panel

Robot lower arms: 2 meters by 4 meters.
Drawing of lower arms: 2cm by 4 cm.

Robot feet: 2 meters by 4 meters.
Drawing of feet: 2 cm by 4 cm.

Add some interesting details to your
SCALE DRAWING of a robot.

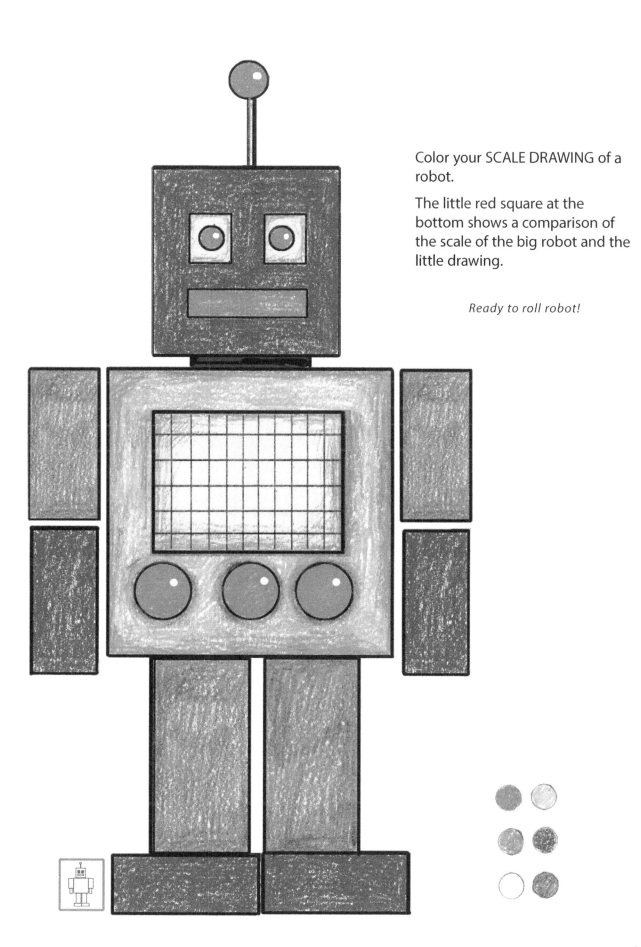

Color your SCALE DRAWING of a robot.

The little red square at the bottom shows a comparison of the scale of the big robot and the little drawing.

Ready to roll robot!

Scale Drawing Using A Grid

You can use a GRID to make drawings larger or smaller. When you copy a drawing and change the size, you are changing the SCALE.

To begin, make two grids. The first is the small grid and the second larger grid will SCALE UP your drawing.

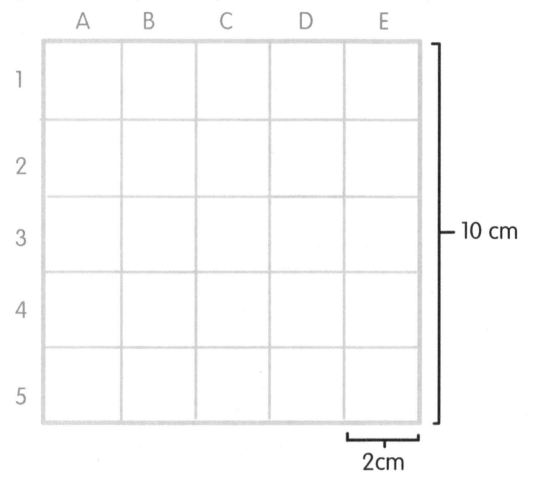

Draw a small GRID that is 10 cm by 10 cm. Mark off 2 cm sections. There will be five squares across and five squares down.

Label the squares A through E across the top, and 1 through 5 along the side. This will allow us to name the squares and keep track of the placement of the drawing.

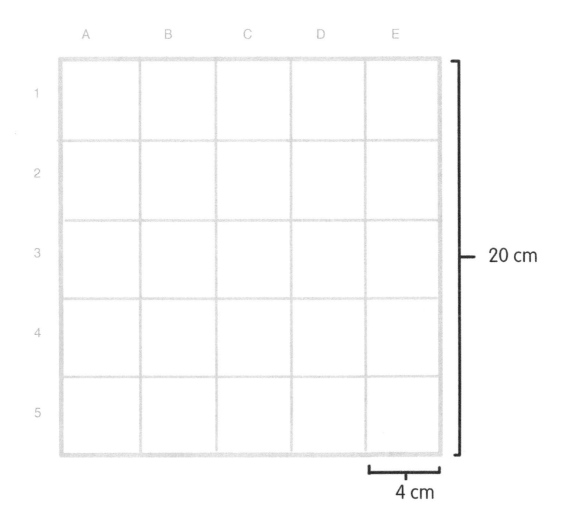

Create a second grid that is 20 cm by 20 cm. Mark off squares at 4 cm intervals. There will be five squares across and five squares down.

Label the squares the same as the smaller grid: A through E across and 1 through 5 along the side.

The big GRID is the same as the small GRID.

The only thing that has changed is the SCALE.

Here is a drawing of a dinosaur on the smaller GRID. This will be transferred, square by square, to the larger GRID. The drawing of the dinosaur will be exactly the same but it will be larger in SCALE.

Look at the lines forming the dinosaur's head in the smaller GRID. The head is drawn over several squares: 1A, 1B, 2A, and 2B. Look at each drawn line and copy its position in the larger GRID.

Copy one square at a time, looking carefully at the position of the lines in the smaller GRID.

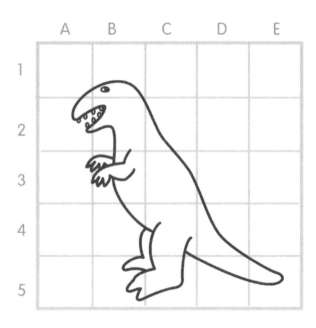

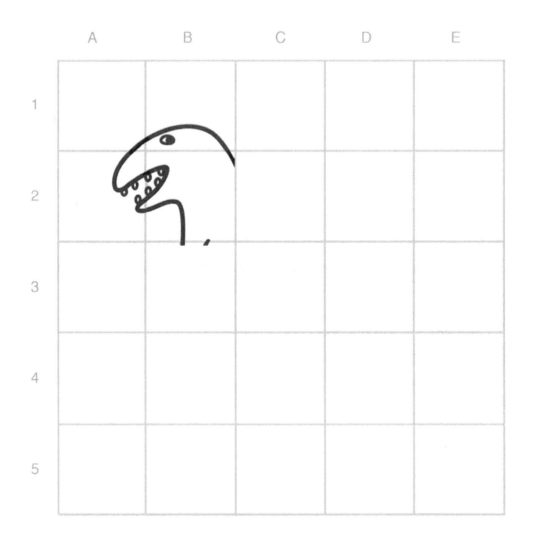

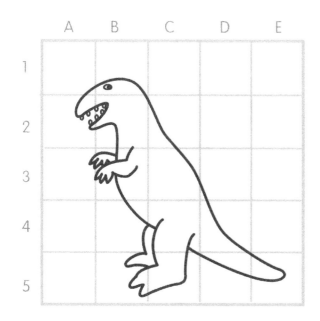

The front legs of the dinosaur are in squares 3A and 3B

Look at the lines in each square in the small GRID and draw them in the larger GRID. Continue to draw each square, one by one, copying the lines you see. Look carefully at the positions of the lines in each square.

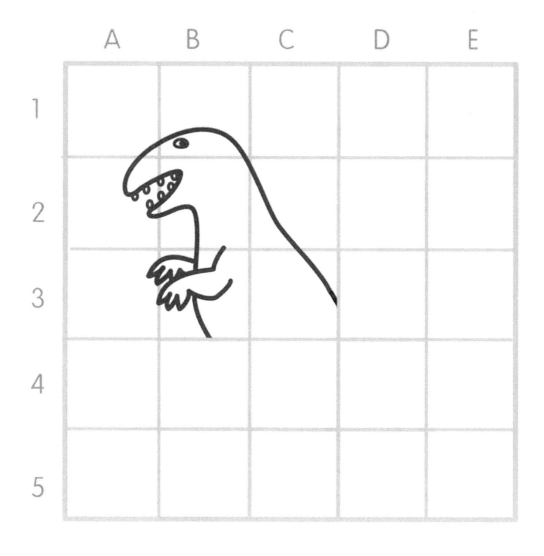

Finish the drawing with the dinosaur's tail. Look at the positions of the lines in each square.

The dinosaur on the larger GRID is the same as the dinosaur on the smaller grid. Only the SCALE has changed.

Dynamite Dinosaur!

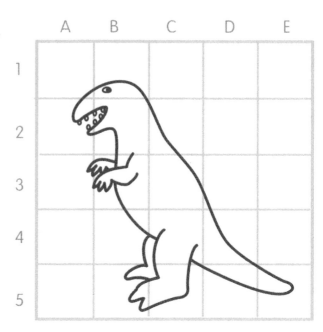

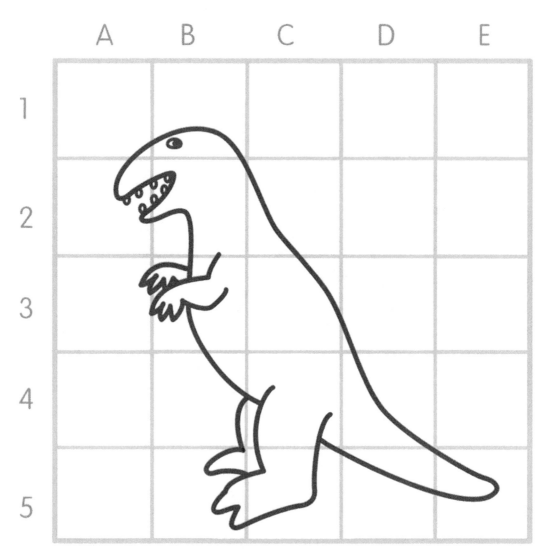

Ratio

A RATIO is a comparison of two numbers. It is a way to compare two amounts or sizes.

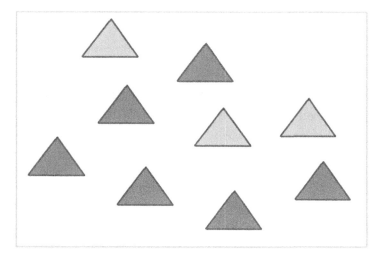

If you have three blue triangles and you also have six red triangles, you have two red triangles for every one blue triangle. This can be expressed as a fraction: 6/3.

R

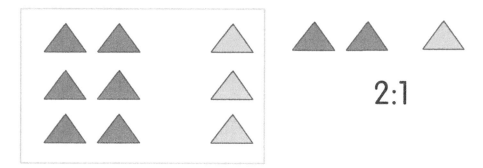

educe the fraction to 2/1. The RATIO of red triangles to blue triangles is 'two to one.' This is also written 2:1.

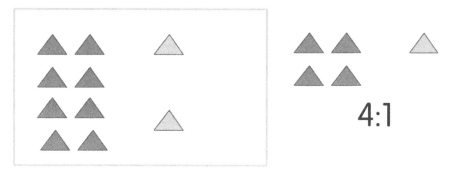

If there were eight red triangles and two blue triangles, we could say that the ratio of red triangles to blue triangles is 'four to one.'

Let's draw a picture using RATIO.

First draw a flying saucer. Start with an oval. Add a curved line to the bottom of the oval. Draw a half sphere on the top of the oval.

Erase extra lines, add windows and an antenna. Color your flying saucer.

Let's also draw an alien. Start with an oval. Draw eyes, ears and a mouth. Add a body and two buttons.

Draw an antenna and two arms. Add to legs and feet. Color your alien.

Draw a picture of six aliens and three flying saucers.
Add a background.

There are six aliens and three flying saucers. The fraction 6/3 can be reduced to 2/1. The ratio of saucers to aliens is 2:1.

How many aliens are there for each flying saucer?

The Golden Rectangle

The ancient Greeks were amazing mathematicians and we owe much of our understanding of basic mathematics to them. Among other things, they discovered some interesting properties of certain kinds of rectangles.

Rectangles can be any shape or size as long as all corners are 90 degrees and both pair of sides are of equal length. You can have tall, thin rectangles, short squat rectangles, vertical, or horizontal rectangles.

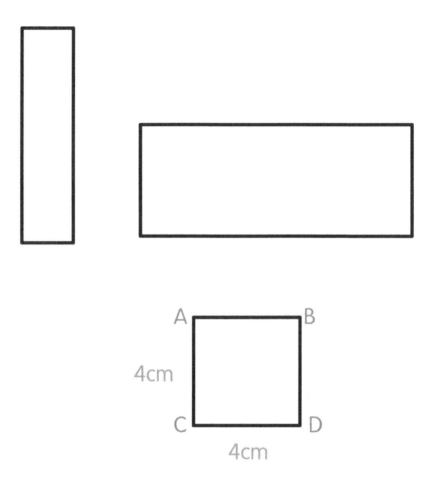

But the Greeks had a favorite rectangle called THE GOLDEN RECTANGLE. The sides of this rectangle had a ratio of 1:1.618.

The length of the long side was approximately 1.6 times the length of the short side.

Let's draw a GOLDEN RECTANGLE. Draw a square that is 4 cm by 4 cm.

Label the corners: A. B, C, D as shown.

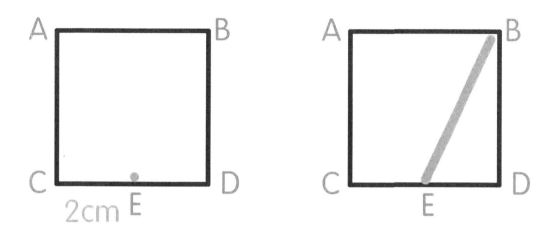

Find the center of side CD by measuring 2 cm from point C. Make a dot and label it E.

Draw a line from point E to point B.

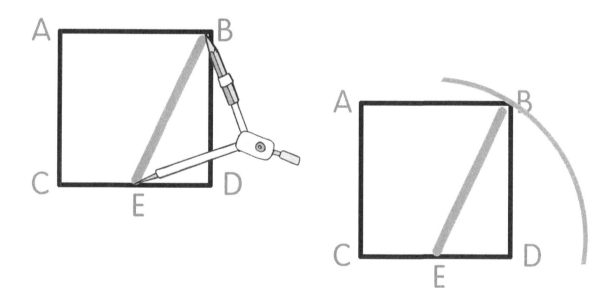

Place your compass point on E and place the pencil on point B.

Line EB becomes the radius of a circle.

Using your compass and pencil, draw a curved arc line.

Extend lines AB and CD to meet the curved line of the arc.

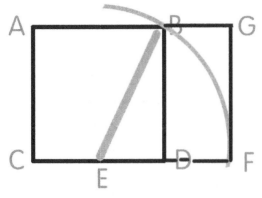

Label these points G and F.

Draw a vertical line to connect G and F.

You now have a rectangle that is 4 cm by 6 cm. Divided by 4 it's 1.5.

The ratio of 4 to 6 is 1:1.5 which is very close to the ideal GOLDEN RECTANGLE.

The Golden Rectangle has many names: Golden Section, Golden Mean, or the Golden Ratio. The greek letter "Phi" is a symbol for this ratio.

Many artists and architects have employed the Golden Rectangle to give pleasing proportions to their work.

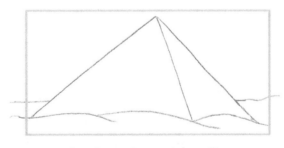

The Great Pyramid at Giza

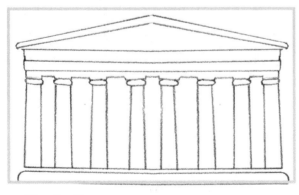

The Parthenon

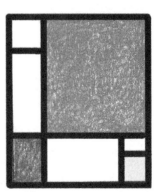

Mondrian's abstract paintings

Can you create a drawing using the proportions of the Golden Rectangle plus other concepts presented in this book?

Have fun! Color your creations any way you like.

MATH-tastic!!!!

Fibonacci Spiral

As you explore more, you'll find that math can help you draw spiral shapes that occur in nature.

Using a graph, draw squares following the Fibonacci sequence of 1-1-2-3-5-8.

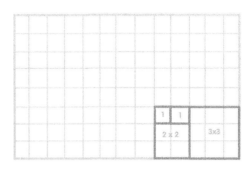

Start by outlining the 1X1 squares, the 2X2, and the 3X3.

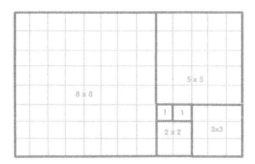

Now add the 5X5 square above and the 8X8 square to the left.

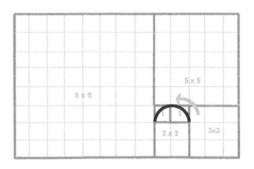

Draw an arc through the 1X1 squares.

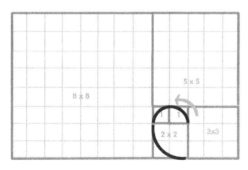

Continue through the 2X2 square...

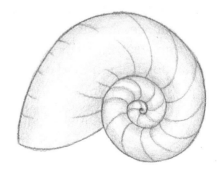

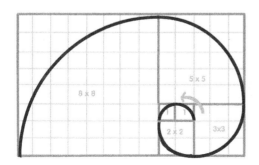

...then the 3X3, 5X5, and 8X8 as well.

Can you see how this pattern works in a shell? Can you think of other objects in nature that are formed with spirals?

63

If you've enjoyed *Draw Plus More Math*
check out these other titles in the series

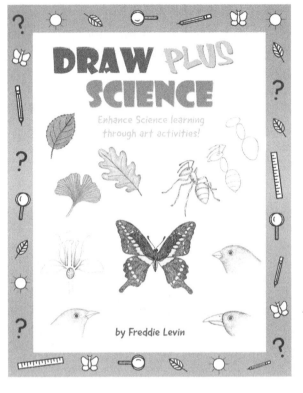

Recommended for younger grades, the concepts you'll find inside include numbers and counting, adding and subtracting, relative amount, sets or groups, one to one correspondence, shapes, symmetry, patterns, sorting, relative position, sequence, fractions, graphs and data analysis.

With an emphasis on observation and information, these drawing lessons are based on concepts which include Classification, Measuring and Recording, Life Cycles, Seasons, Variety in Nature, Climate, Adaptations, Inherited Traits, and Characteristics of Organisms.

Made in the USA
Las Vegas, NV
10 May 2024

89770884R00037